What Is Judaism?

Ernest Brazzos

IN ASSOCIATION WITH

Published in 2026 by Britannica Educational Publishing (a trademark of Encyclopædia Britannica, Inc.) in association with The Rosen Publishing Group, Inc.
2544 Clinton Street, Buffalo, NY 14224

Copyright © 2026 by Encyclopædia Britannica, Inc. Britannica, Encyclopædia Britannica, and the Thistle logo are registered trademarks Encyclopædia Britannica, Inc. All rights reserved.

Rosen Publishing materials copyright © 2026 The Rosen Publishing Group, Inc. All rights reserved.

Distributed exclusively by Rosen Publishing.
To see additional Britannica Educational Publishing titles, go to rosenpublishing.com.

All rights reserved. No part of this book may be reproduced in any form without permission in writing from the publisher, except by a reviewer.

Portions of this work were originally authored by Michael Hessel-Mial and published as *Judaism*. All new material in this edition was authored by Ernest Brazzos.

Editor: Greg Roza
Book Design: Michael Flynn

Photo Credits: Cover ungvar/Shutterstock.com; (series background) Dai Yim/Shutterstock.com; p. 4 Kurka Geza Corey/Shutterstock.com; p. 5 Serhii Khomiak/Shutterstock.com; p. 6 Billion Photos/Shutterstock.com; p. 7 jorisvo/Shutterstock.com; p. 8 Perachel paz Mark/Shutterstock.com; p. 9 Ilya Zuskovich/Shutterstock.com; p. 11 (top) https://commons.wikimedia.org/wiki/File:Temple_Beth_Zion.jpg; p. 11 (bottom) https://commons.wikimedia.org/wiki/File:Joshua_passing_the_River_Jordan_with_the_Ark_of_the_Covenant_(cropped).jpg; p. 12 New Africa/Shutterstock.com; p. 13 artaxerxes_longhand/Shutterstock.com; p. 14 https://commons.wikimedia.org/wiki/File:Thank_offering_unto_the_Lord.jpg; p. 15 ChameleonsEye/Shutterstock.com; p. 17 (top) Ekaterina Lin/Shutterstock.com; p. 17 (bottom) Romolo Tavani/Shutterstock.com; p. 19 (top) Marshalik Mikhail/Shutterstock.com; p. 19 (bottom) Lois GoBe/Shutterstock.com; p. 20 Renata Sedmakova/Shutterstock.com; p. 21 Adam Jan Figel/Shutterstock.com; p. 22 John Theodor/Shutterstock.com; p. 23 MICHAEL HATZALAM/Shutterstock.com; p. 24 Cinematographer/Shutterstock.com; p. 25 Finist4/Shutterstock.com; p. 26 https://commons.wikimedia.org/wiki/File:AnneFrank1940_crop.jpg/Shutterstock.com; p. 27 enesdigital/Shutterstock.com; p. 28 https://commons.wikimedia.org/wiki/File:UN_Palestine_Partition_Versions_1947.jpg; p. 29 Mr_Karesuando/Shutterstock.com.

Cataloging-in-Publication Data
Names: Brazzos, Ernest.
Title: What is Judaism? / Ernest Brazzos.
Description: New York : Britannica Educational Publishing, in association with Rosen Educational Services, 2026. | Series: Discover more: world religions | Includes glossary and index.
Identifiers: ISBN 9781641904674 (library bound) | ISBN 9781641904667 (pbk) | ISBN 9781641904681 (ebook)
Subjects: LCSH: Judaism--Juvenile literature.
Classification: LCC BM573.B74 2026 | DDC 296--dc23

Manufactured in the United States of America

Some of the images in this book illustrate individuals who are models. The depictions do not imply actual situations or events.

CPSIA Compliance Information: Batch #CSBRIT26. For further information contact Rosen Publishing at 1-800-237-9932.

Contents

Chosen People 4
Beliefs of Judaism. 6
What Is a Synagogue? 10
High Holidays 12
The Pilgrim Festivals 14
Other Jewish Holidays. 16
Special Celebrations 18
Jewish History 20
Scattering of People 22
Jewish Movements 24
Anti-Semitism and the Holocaust 26
Modern Israel 28
Glossary 30
For More Information 31
Index 32

Chosen People

Judaism is one of the world's oldest religions. Like Christianity and Islam, Judaism is a **monotheistic relgion**. Jews believe that God chose them to have a special relationship with him. They must devote themselves to God in all aspects of their lives because God selected them to bring knowledge of him to the rest of the world. They believe that, in return, God has promised to make the Jews a great nation that will eventually draw other nations together in a worldwide community of justice and peace. Today, Judaism has more than 14.7 million followers worldwide.

A synagogue is a place where Jewish people gather to pray and worship God.

A mezuzah, shown here, is a small case that holds quotes from the Jewish Bible, including part of the Shema. Jews hang mezuzahs in doorways and on gates.

Twice a day, Jews around the world say a prayer called the Shema. It starts, "Hear, O Israel, the Lord is our God; the Lord is One." This prayer is an important statement of faith in the religion of the Jewish people.

WORD WISE
MONOTHEISTIC RELIGIONS TEACH THE BELIEF THAT THERE IS ONLY ONE GOD, RATHER THAN MANY GODS OR NONE AT ALL.

Beliefs of Judaism

The Hebrew Bible, or the Torah, is the sacred book of Judaism. The first five books of the Torah are especially important. The Hebrew Bible also contains books of the prophets and collections of poetry, stories, and history. The Torah tells the story of the creation of the world. It also explains and interprets God's laws, including the Ten Commandments. Jews believe that God gave these rules to the prophet Moses.

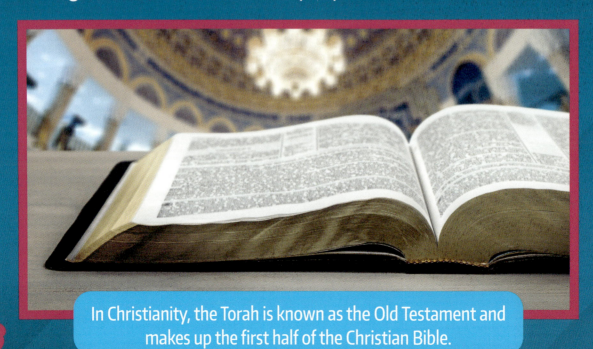

In Christianity, the Torah is known as the Old Testament and makes up the first half of the Christian Bible.

The Torah says that God revealed his Ten Commandments to the prophet Moses, who then shared them with the people.

The Ten Commandments are the most important laws in Judaism. These rules say that there is one God and describe how to treat others. For example, they forbid stealing, killing, or lying. The Ten Commandments also tell Jews to rest on the Sabbath to remember when God rested after creating the world. On the Sabbath Jews pray and eat special meals. Work is not allowed. Jews observe the Sabbath from sunset on Friday to sunset on Saturday.

Consider This

Judaism does not allow people to worship statues or images of God. What are ways to show faith in God that do not involve statues or images of him?

Some Jewish laws forbid bad behavior, while others require good deeds. Some laws forbid certain foods, such as pork or shellfish, and explain how foods should be prepared. The Talmud is a collection of ancient Jewish teachings.

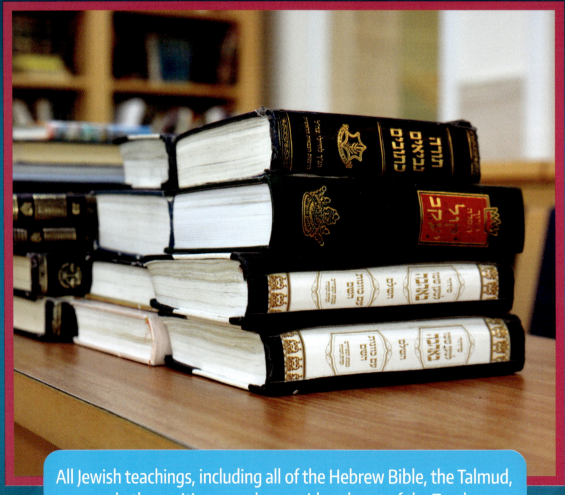

All Jewish teachings, including all of the Hebrew Bible, the Talmud, and other writings, can be considered part of the Torah.

Some Jews pray by reading from a prayer book called a siddur.

Jewish leaders, called rabbis, wrote down those teachings long ago and added their own stories and comments. The Jewish prayer book, or siddur, contains prayers that Jews recite daily. In Hebrew, the word Torah means "to teach" or "to show the way."

compare and contrast

Judaism has many unwritten teachings and customs that Jews follow. They were passed down by word of mouth. How is an unwritten custom different from or similar to a written law?

What Is a Synagogue?

A synagogue is the place where a Jewish community gathers to pray and study. A synagogue is sometimes called a temple or a shul, which is a Yiddish word meaning "school."

The leader of a synagogue is called a rabbi, which means "my teacher." A rabbi provides guidance to the Jewish community. Some synagogues also have a cantor. A cantor is a specially trained singer who leads prayer.

Worship services take place on Friday nights (the beginning of the Sabbath), on Saturday mornings and afternoons, and on Monday and Thursday mornings. Special worship services also take place on holy days and festivals.

The most important part of a synagogue is the ark, or cabinet, that holds the Torah scrolls. A synagogue also has a platform called a bimah, where a reader reads the Torah to worshippers. The main part of synagogue worship is the reading of the Torah. Many synagogues read the entire Torah in one year.

This synagogue, Temple Beth Zion in Buffalo, New York, has a modern design. It has 10 sides, one for each of the Ten Commandments.

compare and contrast

How are synagogues similar to other places of worship, like a mosque or a church? How are they different?

The Torah mentions an "Ark of the Covenant" several times. It is believed to be a storage chest made by Moses to hold God's Ten Commandments. Historians aren't sure if it really existed or not.

High Holidays

The High Holidays are Rosh Hashana and Yom Kippur. Rosh Hashana is the Jewish New Year. The holiday is celebrated in either September or early October. This joyous celebration marks the anniversary of the creation of the world. People gather with family and friends and eat meals with sweet foods, including apples and honey. People go to the synagogue to pray. Prayers include the sounding of the shofar, a trumpet made of a ram's horn. Rosh Hashana begins a ten-day period called the High Holy Days, or the Days of Awe, that ends on Yom Kippur. During this period, Jews think about how to live better lives in the year to come.

The shofar, shown here, is used in prayers before and during Rosh Hashana.

The Torah says that Rosh Hashana and Yom Kippur are days of rest. Jews are not allowed to work during the High Holidays.

Yom Kippur is the holiest day in Judaism. This holiday is called the Day of **Atonement**. It is observed with prayer and fasting. The holiday's purpose is to purify the individual and community. On Yom Kippur, Jews are forgiven for their sins against God. They also ask for forgiveness from people they have hurt. Some Jews wear a special white robe on Yom Kippur to symbolize their purity as they ask God for forgiveness.

WORD WISE
ATONEMENT IS THE ACT OF MAKING UP FOR AN OFFENSE OR WRONGDOING.

The Pilgrim Festivals

The Pilgrim Festivals celebrate both historical and agricultural or seasonal events. These holidays are Passover, Shavuot, and Sukkoth. Passover celebrates the freedom of Jews from slavery in ancient Egypt. The festival of Passover is one of great joy. It takes place for about one week in March or April. Families eat a special meal called a seder. Before the meal the story of Passover is told. The most important food of the holiday is matzo, which is a flat bread made with only flour and water. This reminds the Jews of the bread their ancestors, called Israelites, took with them when they fled Egypt for freedom. They did not have time to let it rise because they were in a hurry to leave.

These holidays are called pilgrim festivals because at one time long ago adult male Jews were required to make a pilgrimage, or trip, to Jerusalem with an offering of crops they had grown.

This Jewish couple is preparing a shelter in which to celebrate Sukkoth.

Sukkoth is an autumn festival that observes the time when the Israelites wandered through the desert. Many Jews put up sukkoth (huts or shelters) and pray and eat their meals inside them to honor the traditions of ancient Judaism. Shavuot commemorates God giving the Torah to the Jewish people.

Consider This

On Passover Jewish families eat a meal called a seder. Matzo, hardboiled eggs, bitter herbs, and other special foods are eaten. Are there meals your family eats on special occasions? Are they religious meals or another kind of celebration?

Other Jewish Holidays

Purim celebrates a time when Jews in ancient Persia (now Iran) escaped a plot to harm them. Purim usually falls in late February or early March. On Purim, Jews go to a synagogue and listen to the story of how Queen Esther convinced the Persian king to stop a plot to kill all the Jews in Persia.

Hanukkah is known as the Festival of Lights. It lasts for eight nights and usually occurs in December. Hanukkah commemorates a military victory long ago. In ancient times, foreign leaders took over the Temple in Jerusalem and tried to make the Jews give up their religion. The Jews defeated the foreign rulers and took back the Temple. According to tradition, the Jews only had a small jar of oil for the Temple's lamps. Miraculously, the oil lasted for eight nights.

During Purim, Jewish families eat together, exchange gifts of food, and dress in costumes. Many families also give to the poor.

compare and contrast

Hanukkah happens around the same time of year as Christmas and Kwanzaa. How are these holidays the same as or different from each other?

To honor the Jewish victory, Jewish families light candles on a special candle holder called a menorah. The eight candles represent the eight nights in the Temple. Gift giving is another part of this eight-day holiday.

Special Celebrations

There are many Jewish ceremonies that occur at special times of a person's life. These include birth, coming of age, marriage, and death. Shortly after birth, a ceremony takes place in which babies are dedicated to God and named. There is a special ceremony called a bris for male infants.

In Judaism, a boy reaches adulthood on his thirteenth birthday, when he accepts responsibility for following the commandments. This ritual is called a Bar Mitzvah. A boy studies the Torah to prepare for his Bar Mitzvah. During a religious service at the synagogue, the boy reads from the Torah in Hebrew. After the ceremony, many families choose to have a party to celebrate the event with friends and relatives. There is a similar celebration for girls, called a Bas, or Bat, Mitzvah.

Bas Mitzvahs and Bar Mitzvahs are usually followed by a fun party to celebrate the girl's or boy's special day.

compare and contrast

Jewish ceremonies aren't that different from those of other religions. Can you think of other religious ceremonies that are similar to the Jewish ceremonies you've read about?

During a Jewish wedding, the bride and groom stand under a covering called a chuppah. A rabbi often leads the ceremony.

Jewish History

The founder of Judaism is the **patriarch** Abraham. He lived about 4,000 years ago. According to the Torah, God told Abraham to leave his home and take his family to Canaan (modern Israel). God promised Abraham that they would become a great nation in this new land. This promise is called the covenant.

Abraham is an important figure in Judaism, Christianity, and Islam. These three religions are sometimes called "Abrahamic religions."

According to the Torah, Moses parted the Red Sea to allow the Israelites to escape from slavery.

Long after the days of Abraham, his descendants left Canaan because of a famine and went to Egypt. There, they were turned into slaves. Around 1200 BCE, the prophet Moses led the Israelites out of slavery. God instructed Moses and the Israelites to travel through the desert back to Canaan. Jews believe that God gave Moses the Ten Commandments.

In Canaan, the Israelites started a nation called Israel. Israel became powerful under its first three kings: Saul, David, and Solomon. David made Jerusalem the capital city. In the 900s BCE, David's son, Solomon, built the first Temple of Jerusalem.

WORD WISE
A PATRIARCH IS THE FATHER OF A FAMILY. A MATRIARCH IS THE MOTHER OF A FAMILY. IN JUDAISM, SEVERAL MEN AND WOMEN CALLED PATRIARCHS AND MATRIARCHS WERE IMPORTANT FIGURES IN THE EARLY HISTORY OF THE JEWISH PEOPLE.

Scattering of People

Babylonians destroyed the Temple of Jerusalem in the 6th century BCE and took control of Israel. After this, many Israelites left. This was the beginning of the Jewish diaspora, or the scattering of Jewish people throughout the world. Some Jews later returned to their homeland and rebuilt the Temple. But the land of Israel continued to be ruled by one foreign power after another. In 70 CE the Romans destroyed the second Temple.

Today, one wall of the Temple is Jerusalem is still standing. It is called the Western Wall, and it is a major religious location for Jewish pilgrims to visit.

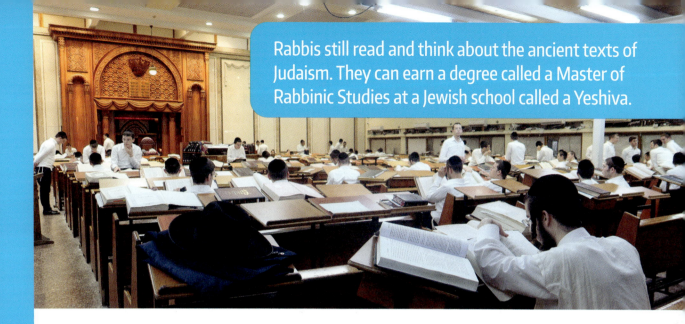
Rabbis still read and think about the ancient texts of Judaism. They can earn a degree called a Master of Rabbinic Studies at a Jewish school called a Yeshiva.

During this time, religious scholars called rabbis became leaders of different Jewish communities. Their teachings were written down so that Jews could follow religious law no matter where they lived. These laws provide guidance on all aspects of life, including food, clothing, business, and prayer.

Over time, the Jewish people spread out to live in many different countries. Most Jews live in Israel and the United States. However, people practice Judaism in many countries all over the world.

WORD WISE
THE ANCIENT BABYLONIANS WERE PEOPLE WHO LIVED IN THE AREA THAT IS TODAY CALLED IRAQ.

Jewish Movements

Many Jewish movements came about due to the diaspora. Because Jews had dispersed to many different areas, the often developed different religious, cultural, and political goals. One movement called Kabbala began in the twelfth century CE. Its believers wanted to know God directly by finding secret meanings in the Torah. A rabbi developed a form of Jewish **mysticism** called Hasidism in the eighteenth century. Hasidism seeks God in everyday life and places great value on righteous people.

Hasidic Jews have very strict customs. They are expected to wear special clothes, cut their hair a certain way, and understand Yiddish, a mixture of Hebrew and Germanic languages.

In recent times, more women have become rabbis.

Judaism has three main divisions. Orthodox Jews are the most traditional. They believe that Judaism should be practiced today just as it was in ancient times. In the nineteenth century two groups broke away to make changes. Conservative Jews uphold many old traditions but have made some changes in their religious practices. Reform Jews made the most changes. They changed Judaism's laws to make them more modern.

WORD WISE
MYSTICISM IS THE EXPERIENCE OF SPIRITUAL UNION OR DIRECT COMMUNICATION WITH GOD.

Anti-Semitism and the Holocaust

After the diaspora, Jewish people living in different parts of the world were often seen as different. They faced anti-Semitism in many places. This means that people did not like them and treated them badly. Many Jews weren't allowed to have certain jobs or to live in certain places.

A young Jewish girl named Anne Frank hid with her family for two years before the Nazis captured them. Frank kept a diary during this time that tells part of their story.

People can visit several camps in Germany where many Jews were held captive during the war and eventually killed. They are now museums and memorials to the dead. They remain chilling reminders of a dark era in world history.

In 1933 a leader named Adolf Hitler took control of Germany. Hitler's political party, called the Nazi Party, hated Jewish people. It tried to make life hard for them. Jews could not attend school or own businesses. Later, during World War II, the Nazis decided to kill as many Jews as possible. By the end of the war, in 1945, more than six million Jewish men, women, and children had been killed throughout Europe. This massacre is called the Holocaust.

The Holocaust came to an end when the Allies—the United States, France, Great Britain, and the Soviet Union—defeated Germany. Today, many countries have Holocaust Remembrance days to honor the victims. World War II and the Holocaust are important topics in schools all over the world.

Consider This

Learning about terrible events of the past like the Holocaust can be distressing and difficult to handle at times. Why do you think it's important to learn about them still, nearly 100 years later?

Modern Israel

In many ways, World War II brought the world's Jewish people closer together. Many Jewish people wanted a country of their own in their ancient homeland of Israel. This idea is called Zionism. In 1948, the modern country of Israel was created in an area called Palestine.

This map from 1947 shows the original plan for the countries of Palestine and Israel.

Today, the ancient city of Jerusalem is the largest city in Israel. It is considered the Holy Land for Judaism, Christianity, and Islam.

Many other people had lived in the land for a long time. These people, called Arabs, did not want to give up land that they considered theirs. In 1948 the Arabs went to war with Israel. Israel won the war and gained more land from the Arabs. This set the stage for many years of fighting for control of the region.

Today Israel is a modern country based on ancient Jewish traditions. It is home to about half the world's Jewish population. It is also home to members of other religions.

compare and contrast

How is the modern state of Israel different from the ancient kingdom of Israel described in the Torah?

Glossary

bimah A stand in a synagogue where the Torah is placed.

cantor A trained singer in a synagogue.

commandment An order from God.

commemorate To mark by a ceremony.

Conservative Judaism Judaism as practiced especially among some US Jews that keeps to the Torah and Talmud but makes allowances for some changes suitable for different times and circumstances.

covenant A solemn agreement.

diaspora The spread of a group in different parts of the world.

Hebrew The language of the ancient Jews, written in different characters than the English alphabet.

menorah A holder for candles used in Jewish worship.

Orthodox Judaism Judaism that considers the Torah and Talmud sacred and that strictly follows Jewish laws and traditions in everyday life.

prophet A person who is chosen to bring the word of God to other people

rabbi A leader of a Jewish community.

Reform Judaism A nineteenth- and twentieth-century development of Judaism in which many older laws and practices were changed or given up to make Judaism more modern

sacred Holy; something important to a particular religion.

siddur A Jewish prayer book.

Talmud The writings that declare Jewish law and tradition.

Yiddish A language related to German that is written in Hebrew characters.

For More Information

Books

Aslan, Reza. *A Kids Book About Israel & Palestine.* Portland, OR: A Kids Co, 2025.

Moening, Kate. *Anne Frank.* Minnetonka, MN: Bellwether, 2025.

Websites

Chabad.org Kids
www.chabad.org/kids/default_cdo/jewish/Kids.htm
This fun, colorful website gives kids a chance to learn more about Judaism. It features videos, games, quizzes, and more.

Judaism Facts for Kids
kids.kiddle.co/Judaism
Read more about Judaism, Hebrew texts, and Jewish ways of life.

Publisher's note to educators and parents: Our editors have carefully reviewed these websites to ensure that they are suitable for students. Many websites change frequently, however, and we cannot guarantee that a site's future contents will continue to meet our high standards of quality and educational value. Be advised that students should be closely supervised whenever they access the internet.

Index

A
Abraham, 20, 21
ark, 10, 11

B
Bar/Bas Mitsvah, 18, 19

D
diaspora, 22, 24, 26

F
food, 12, 14, 15, 17, 23
Frank, Anne, 26

H
Hanukkah, 16, 17
history, 6, 14, 20, 21
Holocaust, the, 27

I
Isreal, 5, 20, 21, 22, 23, 28, 29

J
Jerusalem, 14, 16, 21, 22, 29

M
Moses, 6, 7, 11, 21

P
Passover, 14, 15
prophet, 6, 7, 21
Purim, 16, 17

R
rabbis, 9, 10, 19, 23, 24, 25
Rosh Hashanah, 12

S
Sabbath, 7, 10
Shavuot, 14, 15
Shofar, 12
Sukkoth, 14, 15
synagogue, 4, 10, 11, 12, 16, 18

T
Talmud, 8
Ten Commandments, 6, 7, 11, 18, 21
Torah, 5, 6, 7, 8, 9, 10, 11, 13, 15, 18, 20, 21, 24, 29

Y
Yom Kippur, 12, 13